Ezequiel Farca + Cristina Grappin

PHILIP JODIDIO

EZEQUIEL FARCA + CRISTINA GRAPPIN

Rizzoli Electa

07 **Foreword**
    Paola Lenti

08 **Reinterpreting Modern Tradition**
    The Work of Ezequiel Farca and Cristina Grappin
    Philip Jodidio

20 **Barrancas House**

40 **Culiacán House**

56 **Sierra de la Breña House**

64 **Expendio Tradición Mezcal Bar**

74 **The LOT**

82 **Yacht 196'**

92 **Tigertail House**

100 **Maravilla House**

112 **Venice Beach Townhouse**

122 **Magnolia House**

142 **Explaining What We Do:**
     Ezequiel Farca and Cristina Grappin
     respond to questions from Michael Webb

146 **Alena House**

166 **Benetti Mediterraneo 116'**

182 **Roca House**

190 **Lucca Restaurant**

196 **Loca House**

214 **Benetti Crystal 140'**

230 **Vallarta House**

252 **Offices**

Foreword

The design studio Ezequiel Farca + Cristina Grappin and my office work hand in hand and share a deep mutual appreciation.

Their work seamlessly combines design and architecture. Their projects are more than formal exercises and do not represent aesthetics for the sake of aesthetics. Instead, they are imbued with a passion for artisanal work and a focus on natural and ecologically sustainable materials that are chosen for their quality and because they make use of the latest recycling methods.

Ezequiel Farca and Cristina Grappin are conscious that architects and designers must work in a responsible way that reflects respect for humanity and the environment.

Paola Lentl

Tra l'azienda Paola Lenti e lo studio di progettazione di Ezequiel Farca e Cristina Grappin si è creata una relazione di collaborazione e di reciproca stima.

I loro progetti rappresentano un servizio, capace di coniugare in modo coerente design e architettura; non sono soltanto esercizi formali e non si esauriscono nella ricerca estetica fine a se stessa. In essi c'è la passione per le lavorazioni artigianali e un'attenzione particolare sia per i materiali naturali, sia per quelli eco-sostenibili, selezionati per rispondere ai metodi di riciclo più moderni.

Ezequiel Farca e Cristina Grappin, consapevoli della responsabilità che aziende e designer hanno, progettano sempre con grande rispetto per l'uomo e per l'ambiente che lo circonda.

Paola Lenti

Reinterpreting Modern Tradition
The Work of Ezequiel Farca and Cristina Grappin

Philip Jodidio

Ezequiel Farca and Cristina Grappin have succeeded in developing a unique approach to luxury home design in Mexico, as well as interior and architecture designs in California and elsewhere in the United States. Their collaboration involves a careful integration of the often separate disciplines of furniture and object design, interior architecture, and architecture itself; they have developed a holistic approach to these areas, combining them in a number of spectacular projects where there is an obvious continuity between interior and exterior, where natural materials and their texture play a real role, and where references to the creativity of modern Mexico are replete. Rooted in Mexico City, where the firm was created in 1995, they are also present in the United States with an office in Los Angeles, and in Europe with their Milan office. Their muted palette of colors and their sense of spatial transitions and light ensure that they are indeed capable not only of continuing their work in the US and Mexico, but also of branching out even further.

The architects and designers of Mexico have left an indelible mark on the development of modern creativity. Luis Barragán (1902–1988), for example, was the second winner of the Pritzker Prize, in 1980. Trained as an engineer, his architectural skills were self-taught. In the late 1920s, he was involved with Guadalajara's Escuela Tapatía de Arquitectura, which was based on adherence to regional traditions. His work has been called minimalist despite his use of bright colors and affirmed textures. Planar surfaces in stucco, adobe, timber, and water all interacting with the environment of his sites were his favored compositional elements.

From Mexico City and Beyond

These influences and others permeate the recent work of Ezequiel Farca Nacach and Cristina Grappin Flores, respectively born in 1967 and 1988. Farca received his bachelor's degree in industrial design in 1991 from the Universidad Iberoamericana in Mexico City. He went on to obtain a master's in urban planning from the Polytechnic University of Catalonia in Barcelona and an MBA from University of California, Los Angeles, in 2012. He founded his own design firm in Mexico City in 1995, as well as a furniture showroom. Grappin earned a degree in architecture from the Monterrey Institute of Technology and Higher Education. Since 2010, the pair have worked on a number of high-end residential, hotel, and yacht projects that involve architecture, interior architecture, and design to varying degrees according to the circumstances. Farca has retained a close connection to the wealth of ideas, heritage, and forms that Mexico has to offer, although the firm has recently opened offices in Los Angeles and Milan.

The practice of Ezequiel Farca + Cristina Grappin currently employs forty-two people, including architects, interior designers, industrial designers, and a graphic designer. The partners are involved in each of these areas and have regular meetings with the coordinators for each discipline. They both personally have frequent meetings with clients and make site visits. Grappin states, "We consider this to be an important part of our process, being present and aware of every aspect of a project."[1] Farca insists on the coordination of the approach of the office. "We are very much involved in the process together," he states. "I feel that my strength is how to integrate the architecture, the interiors, and the furniture into a coherent whole."

Farca and Grappin recently designed their own offices in the Polanco area of Mexico City. The 3,477-square-foot office has a glass curtain wall that allows workers there to have a feeling of contact with the exterior. A concrete façade and a vertical garden are significant features of the building, which also has surfaces in marble, stainless steel, wood, and Corian. Expressing the design philosophy of the office, there are no walls separating architects from interior designers, industrial designers, graphic designers, or even from the spaces of Farca and Grappin.

[1] Cristina Grappin, interview with the author, June 2018. Subsequent quotations not cited are from interviews with Grappin and Ezequiel Farca in June 2018.

Photographer
Jaime Navarro, pages 11,16
Quin Bisset, page 12
Javier Núñez, page 15

Materials of the Earth

Although staff uses the latest computer-assisted design technology, they tend to go through a rather long process before that stage is reached. Their first and foremost task is to conduct a bioclimatic study of the site, to gain a better understanding of the natural conditions that surround the area and how they can work with nature, not against it. The partners also put a premium on getting to know their clients and their needs. The next step is a series of freehand sketches in pencil, pen, and watercolor to conceptualize the initial design. They also employ models in order to understand and explain the project in three dimensions. Farca says, "From the initial stages of a project, we try to understand what furniture will fit in the areas proposed and how the spaces will connect. Basically, while defining volumes, we are also thinking in the medium and small scale of furniture and objects. After this, our team begins to work on solving the technical aspects of the project while simultaneously considering the interior architecture and design."

When the studio was founded in 1995 by Farca, it was focused on product design and grew from there to tackle interior design and eventually architecture. Farca states, "We believe that this unique professional trajectory has instilled in our work a deep appreciation for all scales of a project—from small objects to large, inhabitable spaces." Each discipline demands a different methodology and approach, and they make this distinction: there are different aspects to consider when designing different scales and functions; some may take more time or demand different levels of expertise. What is certain is that they don't consider any project type to be more important than another. They see them as parts of a whole that must be simultaneously thought of to ensure a holistic result. For this office, which has taken on more and more "global" projects that include the architecture itself as well as the full interiors, their rather unique holistic approach is well suited to giving their work a strong feeling of continuity and a kind of natural serenity.

Although full architecture projects that include interiors are becoming an increasingly important element of the office's work, it is nonetheless reasonable to try to identify the qualities and characteristics of their projects, no matter what the precise context. Cristina Grappin states, "Exploring and discovering the virtues of different materials is ever-present in our design process. Working closely with artisans to find new ways to interpret and employ traditional materials and techniques is also a staple in our work. We believe that, in a world where things are increasingly mass-produced, it is a luxury to be able to take the time and care that such attention to detail requires. We have understood that there is a market for this sort of work, but we do it mostly because, for us, each piece and space that we create has a soul, and we believe it is valuable to continue to explore and push the boundaries of traditional techniques. We choose natural materials because they age well; in a way, they have a life of their own, and they establish a dialogue with the space that they inhabit." Indeed, when Farca and Grappin use stone, wood, clay, and other materials, they consistently strive to employ them in their most natural form, avoiding industrially produced imitations or processed versions. "We are acutely aware that the architecture we design is intended to last, and that time transforms any building. The patina of the passage of time that natural materials take on is uniquely beautiful and further blurs the line that divides interior and exterior, a concept we are also interested in employing in our architecture," concludes Grappin.

Although they do not employ the saturated colors for which Barragán is universally known, Farca and Grappin readily acknowledge that the older master inspires them. Their reasoning in making this reference is of interest in any attempt to understand their own projects. About their Barrancas House (Mexico City, 2014), Grappin states, "Spatially what Barragán does is to create a pathway, with an ambiance that changes as you enter a house. In our Barrancas House you can feel that, not that we would compare ourselves to

Barragán. You change sceneries depending on how you walk around the house. There is also an intimate connection between interior and exterior. A change of scale modifies one's own perception of space. You can have a small garden or patio but the way you connect it to the interior space creates an entirely different environment. This relation can be created visually, even in a cooler climate." The Barrancas House is based on the renovation of a 1970s home. It makes use of volcanic rock, granite, oak, and local plants to create an earthy feeling that facilitates an integration with the exteriors and thus a "sense of unlimited space."

In citing their sources of inspiration, Farca and Grappin do not limit themselves to Mexico. They also reference architects who might be seen as having a rather different approach, such as the minimalist John Pawson (b. 1949) and the powerful Swiss architect Peter Zumthor (b. 1943). Grappin explains that while both have different approaches to architecture, they have learned something from each. "John Pawson is a master of minimalism, and of designing in a subtle, non-imposing way; we love the attention to detail in his interior designs, and also the mix of materials he selects. Zumthor is assertive in his architecture, he proposes bold volumes, and integrates nature in his work. Nature for him is not only a garden but it is also light and voids. Both bodies of work interest us, though our own approach is neither one nor the other, but rather a methodology of our own that works for us and our projects."

Closer to home and to their Los Angeles office, the pair were also inspired by the work of the late A. Quincy Jones (1913–1979). A professor at the USC School of Architecture, where Pierre Koenig also taught, between 1951 and 1967, Jones has been considered a somewhat underrated figure of California modernism, a fault partially rectified by a 2013 exhibition at the Hammer Museum titled **A. Quincy Jones: Building for Better Living.** Farca and Grappin refer in particular to the Brody House (Los Angeles, 1950) and the very modern glass, stone, and steel Gary Cooper House (Los Angeles, 1955), both by Jones. The Gary Cooper House was built shortly after the actor played the role of the Frank Lloyd Wright–inspired architect Howard Roark in the 1949 film **The Fountainhead.** Another indication of the California influences that have played on Farca and Grappin is their comment on the Kappe Residence (Ray Kappe, Pacific Palisades, Los Angeles, 1967): "A building we admire and reference in our own work—everything from the relationship established between interior and exterior spaces, to the use of wood as a predominant material, to the way volumes are stacked upon and interact with one another." Born in 1927, Ray Kappe built his house on a steep, heavily wooded site. He created six concrete tower supports and a bridgework of laminated beams that allowed existing trees and a stream to be preserved. With its glass walls, skylights, interior planes, and cantilevered wooden decks, trellises, and platforms, the house seems to float over its site.

Clearly, parts of Mexico share with Los Angeles a lush natural setting and warm average temperatures. For Grappin, "The relaxed, unpretentious approach to luxury that is seen in California modernism has become a staple in our work. In terms of moods, this is certainly what has drawn us to California and why we feel at home in our office in Los Angeles." She goes on to affirm, "We find that in Southern Californian architecture, the landscape is often integrated into the buildings by opening up the home to private gardens or views, or simply by using a materials palette that mimics the exterior, and this is something we tend to do as well in our own work. We also like clean, sober lines, and volumes present in both interior and exterior architecture that are aligned with what we have done and will continue to do in our own projects."

The Skills of the Artisans

"We have tried to champion work that can be done locally, and to integrate the skills of Mexican workers and artisans," explains Farca. Even as the firm has worked extensively on architectural projects, he has continued to actively design objects, often in direct relation to houses or other buildings. The firm often collaborates with Monica Calderon Studio when working with resin. Some of the significant objects developed by the office include the Academia Chair in natural fiber for the Lake Two House (in collaboration with Jiménez Weaving Workshop, 2016), the Zihua Chair (in collaboration with Cuatro H Wood Workshop, 2011), stone stools for the Barrancas House (in collaboration with Roberto Franco, 2016), a wood lattice for the Sierra de la Breña House (in collaboration with Cuatro H Wood Workshop, 2016), a Talavera clay lattice for the Maravilla House (in collaboration with Casa Uriarte, 2016), a glass vase for Nouvel Studio (2017), or a remake of the famous Series 7 Arne Jacobsen – Fritz Hansen Chair (2017).

Further afield in time and space, the Mexican team also speaks with an almost textural sense about traditional Japanese architecture. The use of materials and the way they age is definitely part of what they admire, as well as the time-honored sense of detail present in traditional Japanese buildings. For Farca, "In Japanese architecture, there is no hierarchy of importance in the attention given to the different scales of a building, and this is something we believe in as well. Quality and beauty should be present in the large and small scales of every project we are involved in. The concept of ritual is also highly present in traditional Japanese architecture and design, and they manage to make each space have a soul, and the connections between spaces take on great significance. Making your way through these buildings feels poetic in a way, and no area is residual, no space unnecessary. Their undeniable connection to nature is also something that inspires us when we design."

The Spirit of a Place

A significant part of the work of Ezequiel Farca + Cristina Grappin is located in Mexico, be it in Mexico City or more recently near the southern tip of Baja Californa at Los Cabos. High temperatures in Los Cabos vary from 77°F in January to 92°F in July and August. Their Culiacán House in northwestern Mexico is subjected to summer temperatures that are frequently above 100°F. The intimate connection that the pair create between interior and exterior in the houses and the hotel work they have done is quite obviously dependent on the warm climate of their country. "It's true that most of our projects are in areas with privileged climates; however, we have also taken on work in areas with more extreme weather conditions, albeit hot weather, as is the case of Culiacán House or our projects in Los Cabos," says Grappin. She goes on to explain, "the fact is that we conduct bioclimatic studies and base the architectural design on the results as a way to ensure that the architecture we design is suitable for the climate that will surround it, be it in a cold, hot, or mild environment. Blurring the lines between interior and exterior is something we're interested in and, in many cases, we have been able to create this connection due to the privileged climates our projects have been situated in. There are ways to do this, perhaps more subtly, when the climate is not as forgiving, and a bioclimatic study is key."

The reference to Los Cabos and its climate is an important one for the office. They have recently carried forward a number of projects there: for example, at the five-star Grand Velas Los Cabos Resort. Their Frida Restaurant there (2016) takes its inspiration from the life of Frida Kahlo, not in the most obvious way, but on the basis of the architecture of her time, including late 1920s art deco in Mexico. This reference to a rich but often little-known aspect of the country's modern history is illustrative of Farca and Grappin's approach, where there is no sense of any displaced pride but rather a will to explore the realities of recent history and design. They also take on one of the best-known works of the painter, the 1939 **The Two Fridas,** which explores the duality of the artist's heritage—her German father on one side and her *mestiza* mother on the other. The

contrasting duality depicted in this painting was translated by the designers through the integration of different atmospheres within the restaurant.

Another recent interior design project in Los Cabos is the large 32,959-square-foot Loca House, where Farca and Grappin made extensive use of wood, copper, natural fibers, and traditional Mexican textiles. Terraces and a central pool create opportunities for an almost continuous connection between interior and exterior spaces. The custom-designed furnishings and unique pieces created by artisans emphasize the willful blend of modernity and tradition that the firm has clearly mastered. Another residence in Los Cabos, the Maravilla House, is due for completion in 2019. Another very large house, measuring over 33,000 square feet, it has a structure made with a series of walls, patios, and water features, including small waterfalls. The walls are intended to firmly connect the house to its site and also to infuse the residence with colors and textures that are combined with the "blue of the ocean and the infinity of the sky." Cross ventilation and a careful analysis of the site further emphasize the intimate connection of the architecture to this place and no other.

The first full project integrating architectural design and interiors completed by Farca and Grappin was the Vallarta House (see p. 230), a 32,000-square-foot residence located in the Pacific Ocean resort town of Puerto Vallarta. The main living and dining area has glass walls that open to a terrace and pool with spectacular views of the ocean. Natural stone and concrete are used in part because their thermal mass passively cools the house in summer. The home's walls and rooftops thus insulate it from heat, reducing the need for forced air, and also serving to integrate the house with the landscape. The furniture and decorative elements of the house were chosen and designed to integrate seamlessly with the architecture, which the architect compares to "1950s-style modernism." Farca expresses his

admiration for Los Angeles architects like Craig Ellwood and Richard Neutra, making the nature of his interest in California modernism clear.

Another interior architecture and design project, the Expendio Tradición Mezcal Bar (Oaxaca, see p. 64), shows their capacity to relate not only to a historic house, but also to the tradition of mezcal which is made from the agave plant. Intended for tastings and the sale of local products, the design revolves around a single open interior space that maintains the façades and structure of the original building. Recycled mezcal barrels and handmade floor tiles are combined with metalwork by a local artisan. Farca and Grappin are not seeking in any way to indulge in a kind of pastiche with this project; the clean lines of the design might bring to mind the influence of art deco once again, but there is a decided modernity that underlies and confirms the references to tradition, both that of the product and of the building itself. It is not an easy task, especially for architects, to accept and genuinely renew an old building, but Farca and Grappin definitely succeeded in that task with the Expendio Bar.

Offices and Boats

Farca and Grappin have also taken on a number of office design projects, including the Rimova Office (Mexico City, 2018) and Asintelix (Mexico City, 2017), which makes use of an unexpected concrete lattice that filters incoming sunlight and actually enters the three-story building. The Asintelix building also includes a central patio and a rooftop terrace that allow employees to meet or rest. The efficient design in these cases demonstrates that the studio is able to transition smoothly from luxurious houses to modern office spaces.

During the time that they developed a large number of projects in the United States, Farca and Grappin opened an office in Milan. The reason for the new office is directly related to work they have done on a number of yachts. One of their clients for interior design work bought a boat from an Italian manufacturer and did not know how to take on its interior design. The pair found this challenge exciting and have since completed five yachts with two larger and more complex projects underway in this area. Farca explains that he sees the goal of these designs to be linked to "The will to live everyday life both on board and at home with the same comfort and without perceiving any difference or constraint, and bringing daily routines on board. There should definitely be a point of contact between the two worlds, as well as with the world of outdoor living." The attention to detail and to materials, albeit perhaps different ones on a boat, are other points of continuity between the residential or hotel work of the firm and these yachts. A boat such as their recent Benetti Mediterraneo 116' (see p.166), which makes use of materials such as Statuario or Sahara noir marble and has a custom Swarovski chandelier designed by Farca, makes clear that they are fully able to translate their overall work method into a very different environment. Here the point is not about relating to Mexican tradition but rather to a luxurious environment that combines the comfort of a home with mobility on the seas. With a division of their firm now specializing in boat interiors, it is likely that the international presence of the firm will continue and develop in the future. Farca also explains that having an office in Milan has been useful for the coordination of an upcoming project in Mexico that is being carried out with a foreign client. Their presence in Europe has made work with this client substantially easier.

Looking to the Future

The other foreign office of Farca and Grappin is in Los Angeles, where their intention has been to create a point of liaison with clients. Farca and Grappin also completed the 4,484-square-foot Venice Beach Townhouse with Hagy Belzberg, and the Alen M Salon in Hollywood (see p. 112).

The challenge of this practice is no longer to prove that they are capable of carrying forward residential, hotel, or office projects in Mexico or the US. They are already looking toward their own future development. Referring to their recent mindset, Cristina Grappin states, "The main development has been to broaden the scope of our design, exploring new scales and typologies, but the underlying principles that guide our style and design philosophy have remained present throughout the entire period of our activity."

Farca explains that the permissions process in Los Angeles has been slow, in part due to the office's painstaking attention to detail. The firm is proposing to offer a very high level of quality, attention to detail, and client-architect relations. Looking at some American competitors in particular, he says, "We have a different approach—more attentive to dialogue and the careful exploration of details." At thirty years of age, Grappin projects a sense of energy in her description of how the office can evolve. "Finding a way to apply our design ideology to different types of projects is an exciting challenge for us. In the future, we'd like to take on more projects, not in a massive way, but in a way that will continue to allow us to be deeply involved in the design process and to pay great attention to details. We would like to have even more variety of project types; for example, we've never designed a museum or cultural center, and that's something we have great interest in."

Timeless Spaces

Farca and Grappin have already undertaken a large variety of projects in the United States, including a condominium in Marina del Ray (California, 2016, interior architecture and design); interiors for movie theater complexes, such as the LOT in Point Loma, La Jolla and San Ramon (2015, see page 74); the renovation of the 1955 Roscamore House (William Krisell, Bel Air, under construction, began in 2016); an interior architecture and design scheme for a new chain of high-end taco restaurants (San Diego, under construction, began in 2015); and two condos in Miami (two units in the Mansions at Aqualina, 2017, and one unit in the Oceana Bal Harbour Tower, under construction). Also completed in

2017 was the interior architecture and design of ProyectosLA (Los Angeles), a cultural platform where innovative Latin American galleries are invited to showcase their artists.

Where future projects are concerned, Farca agrees that galleries and museums, even in Mexico, are the next step for his firm. "The culture of Mexico is rich and there are a lot of opportunities," he says, "but not always very good ideas." Farca also points to the recent development of major international hotels in Mexico, often developed by international groups who do not necessarily focus their attention on Mexican talents. "Insufficient attention is being paid to Mexican architects and designers," he says. "How is it possible to think of high-end hotels with a really Mexican feeling of architecture and design? There is an interesting gap there, waiting to be explored."

Farca and Grappin have established a singular role in the continuum of modern Mexican design, one that they have developed based on their respective specialties (furniture and interior design and architecture). What distinguishes them from many other young firms is their personal sense of attachment to the modern traditions of their country, and above all their form of organization and work, which takes a holistic approach. Because they design both architecture and interiors whenever possible, every detail including furnishings and surfaces participates in an overall view. This holistic approach escapes architects who do not take the time to design so many elements for a single project. From Barragán to Charles Eames, they have retained ways of looking at space, and the work of the former has surely helped to give them a respect for the deeper meanings of architecture. They modestly refuse a direct connection to Barragán, yet start where the master left off, drawing from their native Mexico the spirit of the earth and traditions, now newly modern: the feeling of the stone, a view of the ocean and the sky, courtyards and pools that open to and reflect the sky. Farca and Grappin call on spirits that they name only with hesitation, the ones who shaped the modern world as much as any European or North American. This is their heritage and their legitimacy.

Theirs is work that has a sense of time and space, of the relation between interior and exterior, but it is also one of materials and textures. By employing "natural" materials, which is to say stones and woods that are not the product of an industrial process wherever possible, they introduce the idea of durability to their work, of surfaces that will age with grace. This idea is in fact not frequent in contemporary architecture, where expediency and cost-cutting are the rule. Farca has stated, "The very identifiable elements that distinguish us have to do with timeless spaces and architecture. We believe that architecture is born from a traditional concept that, beyond inventing, reinterprets the way people use it." Farca and Grappin have clearly referred to the architecture of Mexico, but also, extensively, to the high points of California modernism, including some that others have largely overlooked. What they have drawn from these historic examples is not so much a literal stylistic input as a feeling—one where, as they say, modernity and luxury coexist in an unpretentious and open way. They succeed in extracting an essence from these different traditions and locations, a method that can readily be applied elsewhere, of course. The beginnings of the office in furniture design still serve for their interior work, but they have found a path to develop in an organic way from the conception of objects to that of complete environments, inside and out. Here, there is a focus on comfort, but also a real design to enter into a symbiotic relationship with sites and with nature itself. As they have shown in a number of their renovation projects, Ezequiel Farca and Cristina Grappin are not only respectful of tradition but seek inspiration from it, calling frequently on talented artisans who build their own work on a deft combination of past and present.

Barrancas House

Mexico City, Mexico
2014

Scope of work
Architectural renovation,
interior architecture,
interior design,
furniture design
Area 7,750 ft.^{2} / 720 m^2
Floors 4
**Start and completion
dates** 2012–2014
Materials
Volcanic rock, marble,
granite, oak and teak wood
Design team
Ezequiel Farca, Cristina
Grappin, Fernanda de la
Mora
Photographer
Jaime Navarro, pages 21,
25, 27, 32–34
Roland Halbe, pages 23,
24, 26, 28–31, 35–39

The Barrancas House is a renovation project for a home originally built in the 1970s. For the team at Ezequiel Farca + Cristina Grappin, the challenge was to design in a way that would allow the project to be defined by its focus on detail, modernity, and spatial transitions that generate a sense of excitement for users.

To take advantage of the privileged location of the residence, full height windows were installed, bringing in natural light and forest views without compromising the comfort and privacy of the residents. The program includes a movie projection area, wine storage, private gym, two terraces, a pool, and a garden. There are also unexpected multifunctional spaces created with mobile lattices, hidden doors, custom-designed furniture, and lighting with an automated system for different user needs. The selection of materials such as marble, stone, and wood, along with natural colors like dark green and brown, provide an earthy feel that, integrated with the exterior, create a sense of unlimited space. The landscape was designed with plants that are adapted to the local climate, with vertical gardens on the walls. Solar power automation systems for water saving are part of the design.

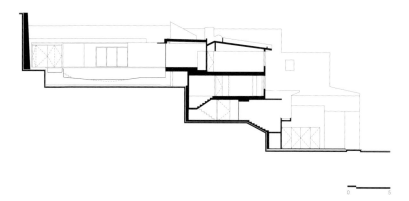

0   5

Culiacán House

Culiacán, Sinaloa, Mexico
2019

Scope of work
Architecture, interior
architecture, interior
design, furniture design
Area 19,375 ft.² / 1,800 m²
Floors 3
**Start and completion
dates** 2015–2019
Materials
Navona travertine marble,
silver-grey travertine
marble, chukum, oak wood
Design team
Ezequiel Farca, Cristina
Grappin, Adria Martínez,
Alonso Pérez, Victor Lima,
Manuel Medina, Michelle
Alfaro, Alejandra Tellez,
José Luis Martínez, Ruben
Martínez, Roberto
Gutiérrez, Nohemí
González
Photographer
Roland Halbe

The Culiacán House is located in the capital of
the northwestern Mexican state of Sinaloa. Due
to the city's year-round heat and high levels of
humidity, a bioclimatic study was conducted and
regarded as a key factor for the architectural design decisions. The home's direct access to an
artificial lake was also a guiding element of the
design. A diagonal wall crosses through the
house, separating the pool house—the main public area—from the kitchen and terrace. The direction of prevailing winds, as well as the views
offered by the lake, dictated that the home should
open toward the south.

The northern side, with no attractive view, was
almost completely closed off. This decision was
part of a conscious effort to separate the structure from its context, allowing the family to feel
as though their home is a private getaway, more
in contact with nature than with the residential
community that surrounds it. Private areas such
as bathrooms and storage spaces were placed to
the north. The bedrooms are on the second floor,
each one enjoying a view of the lake. The materials palette was carefully chosen to envelop the
home in a feeling of warmth and comfort, despite
its large scale.

Sierra de la Breña House

Mexico City, Mexico
2016

Scope of work
Architectural renovation,
interior architecture,
furniture design
Area 7,535 ft.² / 700 m²
Floors 3
**Start and completion
dates** 2014–2016
Materials
Volcanic stone, oak, white
stone façade, teak wood
lattice screen
Design team
Ezequiel Farca, Cristina
Grappin, Adria Martínez,
Manuel Medina, Daniela
Motta, Gabriela Barrera
Photographer
Jaime Navarro

The Sierra de la Breña House is a renovation project for a home originally built in the 1950s that posed structural and design challenges due to its radial floorplan. Several generations of inhabitants had left their own touches on the house, leading to layer on layer of modifications that were removed with the intention of uncovering the essence of the house and returning it to its initial state.

The garden—a generous area that, in addition to providing views of lush greenery, functioned as a source of natural brightness for the entire property—became the guiding element of the renovation, which sought to bring the garden's presence into the home. The building was reconfigured, creating an open floor plan by eliminating walls that separated the home's ground level leading to the garden. The opening of the home as much as possible to its exterior was accomplished with the use of continuous floor-to-ceiling custom-designed windows. On the upper level, a teak wood lattice acts as a filter for sunlight, providing privacy to the users without compromising the indoor areas' relationship with the exterior. Simple, local materials were employed to give this home a clean yet cozy feel. The architects aimed to respect the essence of the home by preserving as much as possible. In this spirit, the façade's original marble was restored. All spaces were designed with a degree of independence so that family members can easily gather or separate, depending on their daily activities.

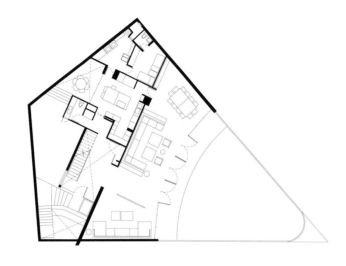

0   5

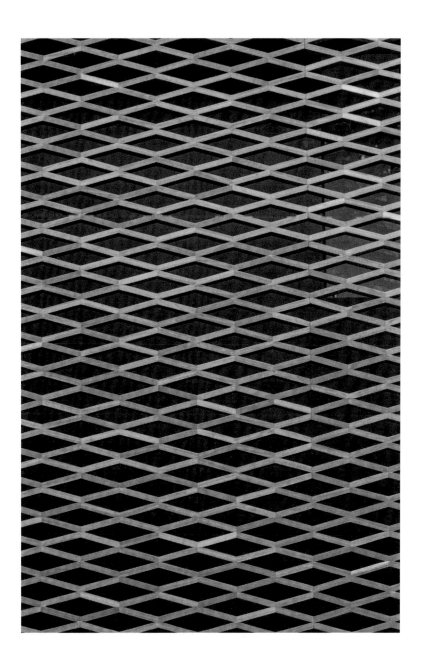

Expendio Tradición Mezcal Bar

Oaxaca, Oaxaca, Mexico
2014

Scope of work
Interior architecture,
interior design, furniture
design
Wooden gate
Francisco Toledo
Area 2,314 ft.^{2} / 150 m^2
Floors 1
**Start and completion
dates** 2013– 2014
Materials
Black clay, recycled wood,
concrete tiles
Design team
Ezequiel Farca, Cristina
Grappin, Ian Castillo
Photographer
Jaime Navarro

The Expendio Tradición Mezcal Bar is located in a historic house in Oaxaca that was transformed to allow visitors to enjoy the traditional local atmosphere, food, and mezcal, an alcoholic beverage made from the agave plant. The Expendio Tradición takes its name from the venues that sold this drink in the past, a concept that the Chagoya family, who has produced mezcal for 140 years, shared with the architects. The program was to convert the interior into a space where everything is designed around the brand. The interior design provides space to accommodate a range of activities, including presentations of mezcal from the region, tastings, and sale of local products that are carefully selected to complete the regional spirit, such as the organic, sustainable foods produced by Villa de Palos.

The design scheme was to create a single open interior space while leaving the original structure of the house and its façade intact. The bar was treated as the focal point. Overall harmony was created with the use of materials such as recycled mezcal barrels, traditional black clay tiles, and handmade cement floor tiles. The use of these materials generated local employment and economic benefits. The original metalwork for the bar was recreated in wood by local artist Francisco Toledo, whose design provides a regional touch. His work, together with that of the Mexico City–based graphic designers Savvy Studio, was successfully integrated with the range of materials to make a coherent whole.

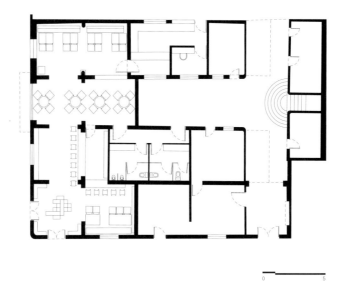

The LOT

San Ramon, California
2015

Scope of work
Interior architecture,
interior design, furniture
design
Area 43,00 ft.^{2} / 3,994 m^2
Floors 1
**Start and completion
dates**
April–November 2015
Materials
Modular carpeting, oak
wood furniture, walnut
wood dividing panels
**Architecture (City
Center Bishop Ranch)**
Renzo Piano Workshop
Architecture (The LOT)
Alta Design Development
Design team (The LOT)
Ezequiel Farca, Cristina
Grappin, Carlos Wellman,
Adria Martínez, Gabriela
Barrera, Adolfo Fastlicht
Photographer
Errol Higgins

Located within a shopping complex designed by architect Renzo Piano in San Ramon, California, this version of the luxury movie theatre The Lot is the fourth that has been taken on by Ezequiel Farca + Cristina Grappin with Carlos Wellman and Adolfo Fastlicht.

As with the other three locations, the intention behind the interior architecture and design was to provide moviegoers with a unique experience that reflects California's traditionally laid-back approach to luxury. In addition to the movie theatres, amenities such as a lounge bar and a fine dining restaurant were a key part of the program, giving the complex a variety of possible activities for moviegoers to enjoy during their stay.

Yacht 196′

Viareggio, Italy
In process

Scope of work
Interior design
Length 196 ft.
Start and completion dates
2017–in process
Materials
Glass, marble, wood
Design team
Ezequiel Farca, Cristina Grappin, Ana Elena Torres
Images
Germán Lomelí

The interior for this fully customized 196-foot motor yacht was conceived with the intention to connect interior and exterior spaces. The design voluntarily blurs the line that separates inside and out through the strategic use of folding doors, seamless thresholds, carefully designed and hidden technical details, panoramic views, and more. The studio envisioned a space free of technical limitations; therefore, the elevator is panoramic, and the technical ducts are grouped and centered in a single space, similar to building design, concentrated within a single staircase. The top deck has been designated as a space for the owner, as opposed to a conventional sundeck. In order to adjust to a gross tonnage study, both indoor and outdoor areas are conceptual. The end goal is to replicate the familiar comfort of daily life in the designed spaces, adapting it to a maritime lifestyle.

The main salon has a Nero Marquina marble ethanol fireplace, and a backlit ceiling with a continuous wooden lattice. A hidden bar in millwork with panoramic windows and works of art has swivel sofas for flexibility of the space.

 The bow area offers a spacious lounge, swimming, and dining area as well as a more private spot. The sky lounge provides a large living room as well as an integrated onyx backlit bar to hold activities for guests of different ages. The aft deck is a relaxing, casual area for dining and lounging while sailing. The owner's deck provides a panoramic view to the forward outdoor deck, which comprises a see-through Jacuzzi and sun pads, and on the aft deck is a private gym that can be opened to the outdoors and provide a leisure area after a workout.

Tigertail House

Los Angeles, California
Under construction

Scope of work
Interior architecture,
interior design
Area 13,239 ft.² / 1,230 m²
Floors 3
**Start and completion
dates**
2016–in process
Materials
Ocean black travertine
marble, basaltine, oak,
calacata marble
Architecture
Belzberg Architects
Design team
Ezequiel Farca, Cristina
Grappin, Adria Martínez,
Fernanda Rodriguez,
Viridiana Quintana,
Images
Germán Lomelí

Tigertail Road is located in Brentwood, not far from the Getty Center. In this area, known for its impressive homes, Ezequiel Farca + Cristina Grappin worked with Santa Monica–based Belzberg Architects. The site, in a gated neighborhood of five homes, originally belonged to the Los Angeles architect A. Quincy Jones (1913–1979). His home burned down in 1955, and an existing structure was demolished to make way for the new project.

The Tigertail House consists of two super imposed and strategically placed volumes. The upper element, with a louvered façade, contains the bedrooms and floats over an informal lounge and kitchen. A volume on the ground floor that functions as a covered terrace framing the wooded landscape was built in wood and finished in matte white plaster. The floors are predominantly clad in travertine, an element that unifies public and service areas and is surrounded by walls that are covered in volcanic stone, establishing a metaphor of a building emerging from the earth. The architects generated a coherent architectural form that is in constant dialogue with its natural context, placed carefully to take advantage of views and generating thermal comfort within the home.

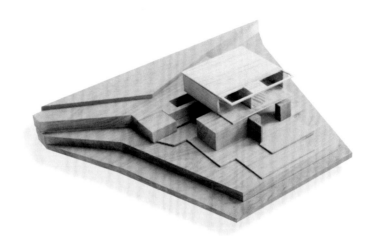

Maravilla House

Los Cabos, Baja California Sur, Mexico
In process

Scope of work
Architecture, interior
architecture, interior
design, furniture design.
Area 33,131 ft.² / 3,078 m²
Floors 2
**Start and completion
dates**
2017–in process
Materials
Concrete, natural oak,
marble, copper
Design team
Ezequiel Farca, Cristina
Grappin, Adria Martínez,
Estelle Bordas, César
Felipe Lima, Alonso Pérez,
Manuel Medina, Alejandra
Tellez, Paola Castañedo,
Daniel Valero, Roberto
Valdez, Viridiana Quintana,
Manuel López
Images
Germán Lomelí

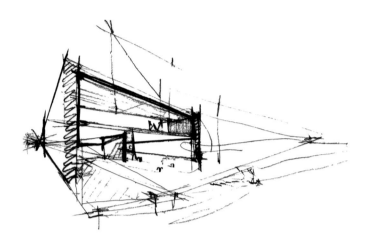

This house is located on an elongated site overlooking the ocean at Cabo San Lucas. A formal scheme was established with a series of large, rammed-earth walls, patios that configure the spaces within the house, and several water mirrors, complete with small waterfalls that create an atmosphere of serenity. A profound connection with nature was initiated though open spaces that introduce natural light and encourage cross ventilation. The use of the earth as a construction material serves to further connect the home to the site, blurring the lines between nature and architecture. The colors and texture offered by this material function as a perfect framework for generous views to the blue of the ocean and the infinity of the sky.

The access has a blind façade where the protruding volume of the second-level bedroom serves as a roof that directs residents and guests through a private patio with a tree and basin toward the main entrance. In the main patio, a water mirror located between two double-height walls of rammed-earth frames and echoes the sky. An untamed, organically grown garden is located on the lateral side. A small incision on one of the earth walls leads to a waterfall, making this a contemplative space. The eastern façade is completely open toward the ocean. The presence of the sun has been modulated with imposing concrete slabs over the public area on the ground floor. Upstairs, the slabs serve as terraces for bedrooms. A pool at the edge of the site marks a thin line that blends into the horizon. The main bedroom has a real connection with the ocean, which can be appreciated from two different angles, as well as a terrace, fire pit, and private Jacuzzi.

Venice Beach Townhouse

Santa Monica, California
2017

Scope of work
Interior architecture,
interior design, furniture
design
Area 4,843 ft.² / 450 m²
Floors 3
**Start and completion
dates** 2016–2017
Materials
Oak floor and Carrara
marble
Architecture
Belzberg Architects
Design team
Ezequiel Farca, Cristina
Grappin, Adria Martínez,
Estelle Bordas, Gabriela
Barrera, Ximena Magaña,
Víctor Burgos
Photographer
Jaime Navarro

This house in Santa Monica was designed to meet the residents' spatial needs and to host their collection of contemporary photographs. The architectural program was divided into three functional levels. The first of these is social or public, the second is private, and finally there is a rooftop garden. The general concept of the house is based on living with the collection, which the owners started more than thirty years ago.

In the main hall, ample natural light fills the spaces through a double-height skylight and a floor-to-ceiling window with a smoked film coating. This lighting configuration is intended to make the collection a protagonist of the interiors. At night a museum-type rail illuminates the perimeter, creating a gallery environment. The interior furniture was carefully designed so that the materials generate chromatic contrasts and form a harmonious and natural integration of space, art, and daily use. The interior floors are in European oak with a uniform tone. The walls are finished in different shades of gray. A terrace leading to the exterior passes near the main hall. An outdoor dining room, and a fire pit add to the public spaces. Here, ceramic glazed concrete floors create a dialogue with the interior. The second level is devoted to private spaces, but the design intentions remain very similar. For the roof garden, the program was extended to take advantage of every available space, and includes a Jacuzzi, deck chairs, a complete grill with a pizza oven, a large dining room and an outdoor sofa with fire pit. Concrete masonry and tall plants on the roof were used as a living visual barrier. The exterior materials of the house affirm a contrasting palette, passing through a range of grays and different natural shades of wood.

Magnolia House

Mexico City, Mexico
2017

Scope of work
Architectural renovation
interior architecture,
interior design, furniture
design
Area 8,245 ft.^{2} / 766 m^2
Floors 2
**Start and completion
dates** 2014–2017
Materials
Veracruz travertine
marble, oak wood, cumaru
wood panels
Design team
Ezequiel Farca, Cristina
Grappin, Jorge Quiroga,
Ana Elena Torres, Gabriela
Barrera, Victor Burgos
Photographer
Jaime Navarro

The renovation of the Magnolia House sought mainly to rearrange spaces and significantly improve its spatial, functional, and formal qualities. This restructuring allowed the architects to improve the home's views, increase the amplitude of the space, and generate a direct connection between the exterior and interior, creating a symbiotic relationship between the residence and its immediate context.

The original space, for which the studio designed the furniture, remained intact for twenty-five years, and the program was no longer adapted to the family's current needs. They decided not only to propose a functional solution, but also to include an art collection and generate a new design language consisting of three living blocks finished in travertine marble. The ground floor includes social areas that are closely linked to the exterior; the private areas are on the upper floor. The blocks are connected through a volume that marks the residence's central axis and includes a double-height space flooded with natural light. New spaces were conceived in relation to objects such as artworks; elements like scale, natural and artificial lighting, and the intention and significance of the artworks were considered. The existing tree mass on the site was used to filter the light in areas too exposed to the sun. Due to the garden's location in the rear, the architects were able to fully open the home without compromising privacy. Bedrooms located on the upper level are continuous and narrow, and bathrooms were placed strategically to have large openings, creating a diaphanous and intimate atmosphere.

The three main materials used for the renovation were wood, marble, and Veracruz travertine. All are present in both the exterior and interior, providing a sense of unity to all areas of the home. Travertine was chosen for its ability to project a neutral tone when seen from a distance and for its porosity and texture, which give it depth and warmth closer in. The wood on walls, ceilings, and furniture creates a sense of comfort that contrasts with the smooth surfaces of desks and fixed marble furniture.

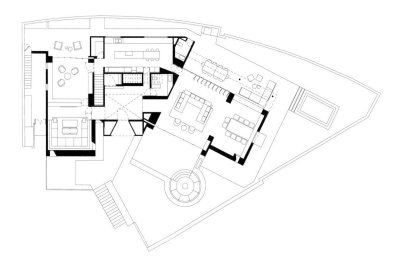

Explaining What We Do:
Ezequiel Farca and Cristina Grappin
respond to questions
from Michael Webb

Michael Webb How did you both get started?

Ezequiel Farca Even with a master's degree I had a hard time getting a job as an architect, so I began designing furniture. My first encounter with serious architecture was through Pancho Gilardi, who had commissioned a house from Barragán. I was twenty-one, and he invited me to his home for lunch. I was alone for five minutes before he arrived, sitting beside the iconic blue pool with the red column, entering the water, and I started to cry; it was as though God was there. When Pancho arrived, he showed me the photos he had taken of my furniture, and over lunch he said something I'll always remember: "In life you have to do things right. There's no other way. I can offer you a space in my studio and we'll have an opening for your furniture." Four months later I had my first introduction to the design world; he was my mentor. I spent the next ten years doing custom furniture. From there I progressed to interior design. One of my clients wanted a second home and asked me to do the architecture. That segued into yachts, restaurants, and hotels.

Cristina Grappin I wanted to study art, having painted since I was a kid, but switched to architecture—which for me is an art and a way of expressing yourself through space. I represent it in paintings and collages; I don't know how to do a rendering. When I got out of school, I worked briefly for TEN and then joined Ezequiel in 2011, sixteen years after he started his practice. I was the only architect there—everyone else was an interior designer—but I loved Ezequiel's emphasis on detail. I felt a design chemistry with his mastery of different scales. Now the balance has shifted; nearly all the forty people in the office are architects.

MW How has the practice changed over the seven years you've been working together?

EF Having two creative minds instead of one makes it completely different. Cristina has brought several things. First, the difference in our ages—her sensibility, as a younger woman, is quite different from mine. I'm strong on practicality and poetic spaces but she has the practical experience. She's better organized and her personality is good in dealing with people. We get together to discuss every aspect of a project. I'm very demanding, and other people may not get it right away—Cristina makes it happen. We share a vision and think in a very similar way but at different scales. Detail and emphasis on function is the same whether it's a 1,000-square-foot apartment or a 20,000-square-foot house.

CG I've learned a lot from Ezequiel in his emphasis on detail, and my approach to architecture is totally different from what it was seven years ago. If you don't pay attention to detail, it won't have soul, and it's not architecture for me. Spatially we complement each other. We do bioclimatic studies with consultants and incorporate the results into the design—how it is going to impact the site and its ecosystem? And there's a lot of industrial design in these projects. Right now it's mostly residential, but I hope that, one day, we can bring the same qualities to a museum and other public spaces. Our goal is to improve lives through design.

MW How do you feel about your roots and culture? Do they impart a distinctive character to your work?

CG Society and culture shape you as a designer. People here are happy with themselves, and try to be innovative and competitive, even though we don't have the same opportunities as in the U.S. and Europe. Living in Mexico, where things work in spite of the chaos, encourages you to find creative solutions. We collaborate with artisans using traditional methods because those are easily available. I think we're at a point where we want to return to our roots, but in a modern way. When we start on an architectural project, we draw organically on our Mexican heritage and identity. You want to strike a balance; to make the client happy and create a building that is part of the social context and natural environment.

EF I agree with Cristina. Thirty years ago, when I started designing furniture, I discovered that all the upscale pieces were imported from Europe, were heavily taxed, and took four months to arrive. That gave me an opportunity. I traveled to international furniture fairs and pushed Mexican manufacturers to match that quality. Once I had demonstrated I could do it myself, people hired me. It's been evolving ever since, creating openings for other designers. The same thing has happened in architecture, where we have become a global player. I design boats for Italian firms from our office in Milan, and I relocated to L.A. five years ago to enlarge our market and make myself accessible to U.S. clients.

MW How do you respond to the spirit of place?

CG On every job we hire a consultant to do a bio-climatic study. This started when we were doing big houses and wanted to integrate them with the environment. Different walls for each orientation conserved energy. Owners were initially reluctant to cover the added expense, but pleased to discover how little they had to use the air conditioning. Our consultant recommended lots of mechanical devices; we prefer to use passive strategies, indigenous solutions, and locally sourced materials—all which conserve energy. When we start our research, we study the regional vernacular, often employing, when it's necessary, a courtyard or breezeways to channel fresh air.

Right now we're doing a house in Yucatán. The client described the look and feel she wanted, showing us pictures of homes in Bali and her New York loft, with its high ceilings and expanses of glass. We had to explain the constraints. Because the site is remote, the workers have to drive an hour, and the roads are too narrow to bring in heavy machinery. That affects the design and the materials; prefabrication and daring cantilevers aren't going to work. She had twenty ideas; we picked the five most important and modified the others. There's a lofty room and the windows are shaded by wooden shutters and a portico. The ocean view and sensation of being outside is achieved but you are protected. She wanted exposed wood, but in that climate it would last only four months, so we took it inside.

MW How do you build a relationship with your clients?

CG It's a long process. We show them pictures of things that work and things that don't and get their reactions. Then we look at the pictures they send us and consider the features they like in each. Every project has a soul and its own personality. We get to know our clients and understand the way they live. Then we create a set of plans and renderings to show them what we propose. What's important is to ask the right questions, make best use of the budget, and understand the site. Thus far we've not had a dissatisfied client.

In Puerto Vallarta, we showed the client the view the house would command. The clients have built houses around the world and they immediately got it. Of course, there were changes over four months of discussion, but they understood what we were proposing and what could be changed. We design simultaneously from inside out and outside in.

EF The most gratifying part of a residential project is seeing families using and enjoying every part of their house. We feel very lucky to be part of the process and deliver a house that will enrich their lives. Most of our clients are referrals, and we often do three or four jobs for the same person. Often the joy lies in a special feature. For the house we are currently building in Cabo St. Lucas, we are adding a rooftop observatory—a shallow bowl where they can lie back and gaze up into the heavens. We employed a similar idea in Mexico City, where an apartment in the St. Regis is oriented toward the angel atop the column in the Avenida La Reforma.

MW Do you offer clients things they never thought of, using their ideas as a point of departure?

CG That's a constant with all our users because we are a young firm and are still trying new things. An exuberant couple wanted a big house in which to throw parties on a wooded plot outside Mexico City. They showed us lots of pictures of houses in Miami and California, and it was a challenge for us to please them while creating timeless spaces they wouldn't tire of. We described the experience they would have in each room. Now that it's done, and they are in love with their home, even though it's quite different from the images they first showed us.

EF Sometimes you have to play the role of psychologist to understand what clients are thinking, which may be quite different from what they are saying. We like to take a holistic approach to our designs.

MW Is it difficult to switch scales?

CG There is a common denominator: all interiors, from a yacht to a hotel, are scaled to human beings. And there needs to be personal interaction with the space. With hospitality you are limited only by the budget and the brand—it's not as personal as a house. The two restaurants we did for a five-star hotel in Cabo St. Lucas had to have a different ambiance—we were given a free hand to make them ebullient. Usually we limit ourselves to two or three materials and a feeling of simplicity; here we could be more elaborate, while keeping it timeless. That was a challenge, but it's become easier as we've done more restaurants and hotel lobbies. We recently did our first office interior, for a client who liked the house we had done for him, and we used natural materials like wood and marble in the 30,000-square-foot space to give it a comfortable, almost residential feel.

EF We have a young client right now who wants an explorer, a boat he could sail to Antarctica for two months. One of the two models he was considering was more stylish but didn't have the capability. Safety is the primary issue. So I customized the design to merge practicality and looks to satisfy both his fantasies. Previous boats we've fitted out have fiberglass hulls that cannot be changed; this is a steel boat, built from scratch like a house. It's an interesting project because we are getting into the bones of the construction and the spaces—including a rear platform for a two-person submarine, which meant that the pool had to be relocated.

MW Do you sometimes advise commercial clients that they need a different concept?

EF The market in Mexico has become more sophisticated—in the city and the resorts. We are currently doing a project with the Waldorf Astoria. They supplied photos to illustrate what they wanted, and we had to tropicalize them to make them work for Mexico. Mexicans have a different culture; typically they go to lunch at 3:00 and they can be at the same table through midnight. So, if the place is too formal, the Mexicans won't go; they are just waking up when Anglos are having their lunch.

MW Do you still design furniture for your interiors?

EF Good design is now available online so it's easier to integrate other brands to enrich the space and make it less homogeneous. The manufacturing process is crucial, so we prefer to buy originals, but sometimes pieces have to be customized. We do provide a lot of millwork and we have assembled a design development team of industrial designers, with two production managers to fabricate custom pieces. We've designed a faucet for Stanza and pieces of furniture for Janus et Cie that are being sold all over the world. If Cassina or Poltrona Frau were to commission furniture from us, I'd be very proud to see our designs going into production and sold internationally.

MW You've had a very productive seven years working together and expanding the scope of your practice. What do you hope to achieve in the next seven years?

CG Experimenting with other typologies. When we started doing hotels and offices, and taking on jobs in Europe and the U.S., we challenged ourselves to work on larger scales and to solve different problems. Now, we'd like to apply that experience to cultural projects.

EF Most new museums are a blank canvas or an architectural icon. We want to design from the inside out, creating an interplay of exterior and interior. A place where visitors interact with the art as they do in a private house.

Alena House

Mexico City, Mexico
2019

Scope of work
Architecture, interior
architecture, interior
design, furniture design
Area 14,854 ft.^{2} / 1,380 m^2
Floors 2
**Start and completion
dates** 2015–2019
Materials
Mocafino marble, Veracruz
travertine marble, walnut
wood
Design team
Ezequiel Farca, Cristina
Grappin, Adria Martínez,
Alonso Pérez, Victor Lima,
Manuel Medina, Michelle
Alfaro, Daniela Motta,
Alejandra Tellez
Photographer
Roland Halbe

The Alena House is a project in which the architects sought to create a home that could coexist with the environment of the area. Built on a steep slope on the outskirts of Mexico City, the house responds to the needs of the client and his family: exteriors and spacious public areas allow them to receive guests, and private spaces connect to the exterior.

One of the main objectives was to avoid cutting any existing trees on the site—the heavily forested area offers beautiful views that became a guiding element of the design, which opens in the direction of the trees. The site's topography dictated the placement of the house, since the aim was to propose silent, respectful architecture that disappears into the landscape.

The residence features two volumes with Veracruz travertine marble cladding divided by two gray walls enveloping a double-height room flooded by natural light that welcomes residents and visitors, as well as a floating bridge that connects the private areas. The public areas, including a terrace and a pool house, are on the ground floor. The upper floor contains the private area, which is also connected to the exterior by two independent terraces.

Benetti Mediterraneo 116′

Viareggio, Italy
2018

Scope of work
Interior architecture,
interior design
Length 116 ft.
**Start and completion
dates** 2017–2018
Materials
Marble, leather, wood
Design team
Ezequiel Farca, Cristina
Grappin, Ana Elena Torres,
Paolo Bartoli, Greta Idda,
Rossella De Luzio
**Exterior styling and
concept**
Giorgio M. Cassetta
Photographer
Quin Bisset

This semicustom 116-foot-long yacht was designed and built taking into account the family life of the owner on board. The architects worked for the third time with the Italian ship builder Benetti. Their collaboration made it possible to customize the vessel to provide the level of comfort, lifestyle, and quality expected by the owner. From an enlarged galley to a fully equipped sundeck, the layout, circulation (including a custom elevator), lighting, furniture, and accessories selection provide intimate and warm spaces for the user. The sundeck has Matrix marble around a custom barbecue grill, bar, and side cabinets.

The materials, color palette, and carefully designed details sustain a high degree of comfort and sense of peace throughout the vessel, indoors and out. The dining area features a custom-made Sahara noir marble dining table that blends with a custom Swarovski chandelier designed by the firm, with the support of Benetti and the manufacturer Cantalupi. The living area, where the TV is hidden by Vitrealspecchi-engraved mirror panels, has a Torino sofa by Poltrona Frau. Three main steps in Statuario marble accentuate the main staircase while glass, stainless steel, and shagreen (rawhide) handrails provide the safest grip and comfort. Statuario and Sahara noir marbles are also used with a leather finish in the master cabin shower.

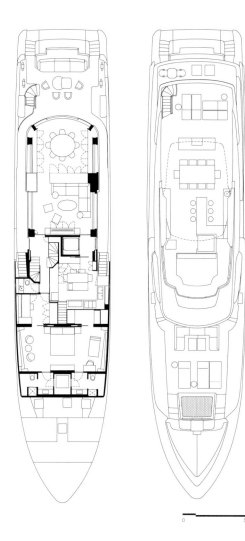

0   5

Roca House

Los Cabos, Baja California Sur, Mexico
2018

Scope of work
Interior design, furniture
design
Area 19,375 ft.² / 1,800 m²
Floors 3
**Start and completion
dates**
January–December 2018
Materials
Ocean blue travertino,
white diocleziano marble,
onyx crystal
Architecture
Ogarrio Zapata
Arquitectos
Design team
Ezequiel Farca, Cristina
Grappin, Paola Castañedo,
Alejandra Tellez, Fernada
Rodriguez, Adria Martinez
Photographer
Adlai Pulido

The Roca House overlooks the Pacific Ocean as well as impressive natural rock formations. Located in Los Cabos, Mexico, it simultaneously offers privacy and direct contact with nature to its users. Within the house, a cool palette of white and silver-grey travertine is contrasted with earthy elements such as teak, echoing a landscape where blue skies and the ocean meet the rocky ochre coastlines.

For Farca and Grappin, the interior design scheme was straightforward. Furniture was custom designed for the house. For the interiors the furniture is mostly in muted tones of grey, with some artworks and accessories in brighter tones to provide color contrasts. Generous windows frame the site's best views in the main public areas which include a large dining room and bar as well as a pool and terrace. The private areas receive natural light through more enclosed terraces. The use of marble, present not only in finishes but in functional elements such as a table-tops and an exterior firepit, establishes a sense of continuity and fluid transition throughout the home.

Lucca Restaurant

Los Cabos, Baja California Sur, Mexico
2016

Scope of work
Interior architecture,
interior design, furniture
design
Area 4,585 ft.^{2} / 426 m^2
Floors 1
**Start and completion
dates**
April–November 2016
Materials
San Gabriel stone, brass,
petrified wood, copper
Design team
Ezequiel Farca, Cristina
Grappin, Adria Martínez,
Gabriela Barrera, Cesar
Felipe Lima, Victor Burgos
Photographer
Jaime Navarro

Lucca is one of the seven restaurants in the Grand Velas Los Cabos Resort in Los Cabos at the southern tip of Baja California Sur. Farca and Grappin approached the creation of this Italian restaurant with a historical vision. In Lucca, a city in Tuscany known for its significant Renaissance architecture, perfection was achieved through harmony and the proportions of the architecture of the time. The aesthetic reinterpretation of Lucca welcomes the user. A series of pilasters organize an arcade of aged mirrors that, together with a tapestry of natural motifs that were an essential feature of the artistic expression of the time, adds drama and depth to the rear of the restaurant. They added a bar that stands out with its wooden finish and then employed lighting techniques that create a contrast within the space, shining from the surfaces and metallic decor in the furniture and accessories.

A series of metal curtains in the middle of the restaurant generates small cores with different environments and a curved layout. An imposing glass wine cellar is on the opposite side of the bar. Combined with the neutral tones of the furniture upholstery, wooden surfaces and the presence of brass in the accessories, floor, and furniture give the restaurant a sophisticated and exclusive atmosphere. This ambiance is transformed for the terrace, with its wooden furniture and a combination of natural materials that evoke traditional Italy, a place that has a special connection with the sea and an outstanding culinary offering.

Loca House

Los Cabos, Baja California Sur, Mexico
2018

Scope of work
Interior design, furniture
design
Area 61,085 ft.² / 5,675 m²
Floors 3
**Start and completion
dates** 2017–2018
Materials
Copper, wood, traditional
Mexican textiles, natural
fibers
Architecture
Ogarrio Zapata
Arquitectos
Design team
Ezequiel Farca, Cristina
Grappin, Paola Castañedo,
Alejandra Tellez, Ruben
Hernández, Roberto
Gutiérrez, Nohemí
González
Photographer
Jaime Navarro

This interior design project is located in Los Cabos, Mexico, where the desert meets the ocean, resulting in warm temperatures moderated by a cool sea breeze. Near the entry, a shallow basin is placed in a courtyard at the heart of the home. A terrace offers a place for relaxation. Lounge furniture in muted shades of white, tan, and ochre surrounds a central pool in an ample lawn that leads to the ocean. The blue of the sky and sea is contrasted with the warmth of the interior material palette. Wood and copper are combined in furniture and decorative elements, while natural fibers and traditional Mexican textiles add depth and texture to the space.

The concept of blending tradition and modernity—a defining characteristic of the work of Ezequiel Farca and Cristina Grappin—is again present in this home. The refined and eclectic spaces contain custom-designed furnishings as well as unique artisanal pieces sourced from around the country.

Benetti Crystal 140′

Viareggio, Italy
2016

Scope of work
Interior architecture,
interior design
Length 140 ft.
**Start and completion
dates** 2014–2016
Materials
Marble, onyx, leather,
wood
Design team
Ezequiel Farca, Cristina
Grappin, Angelique Bidet,
Daniela Gori, Angelo
Longinotti, Salvador
Daniel, Ana Elena Torres
Photographer
Quin Bisset, pages 215,
217, 220, 222, 223
Jaime Navarro, pages
218–19, 224–29
Roland Halbe, page 221

The B-140 yacht is 140 feet long and four decks high. Its program is similar to that of a luxury home, with added technical spaces that allow the boat to sail through the waters its users wish to navigate. Yachts pose challenges that one would not encounter designing traditional architectural spaces. The elevator that leads to the sundeck—a client request that was necessary for the program to function—was a real challenge in terms of engineering and mechanics. Significant changes were made to the basic Benetti Crystal 140': apart from the general layout, several "highlights" were identified to guide the design, such as the use of double-height stairs featuring an illuminated onyx wall and the main cabin's great balcony, which has an automatic mechanism that opens it to the exterior, further amplifying the cabin.

Artisans, carpenters, and the Benetti team played an important role in this project. Additionally, the lighting specialist's participation was crucial, as there were specific details that needed to be enhanced through lighting. Finally, the diversity of materials (marble, onyx, leather, wood) and the broad possibilities they offered, as well as the impeccable work of the artisans who handled them, are aspects of the project that truly stand out.

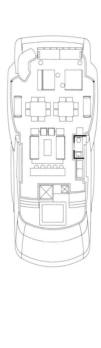

0   5

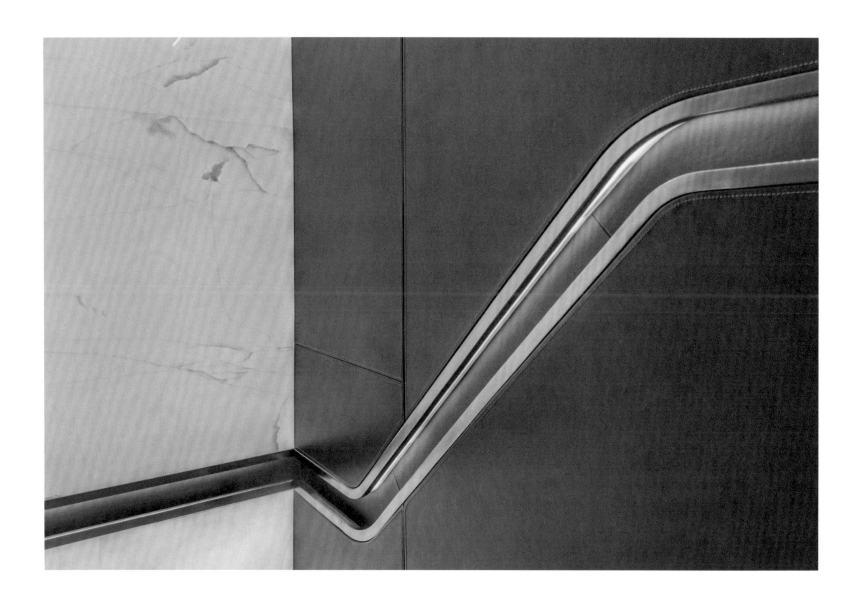

Vallarta House

Puerto Vallarta, Jalisco, Mexico
2013

Scope of work
Architecture, interior
architecture, interior
design, furniture design
Area 32,292 ft.^{2} / 3,000 m^2
Floors 2
**Start and completion
dates** 2011–2013
Materials
Precast concrete panels,
marble, glass, wood
Design team
Ezequiel Farca, Cristina
Grappin, Alejandra Díaz de
León, Fernanda de la Mora,
Angelique Bidet, Michaela
Stachova
Photographer
Jaime Navarro, pages 236,
242–43, 250–51
Roland Halbe, pages 231,
233–35, 237–41, 244–45

Located near the Puerto Vallarta Marina, the architectural design of the Vallarta House centers on bringing the unique landscape of Banderas Bay into the residence without compromising the users' privacy.

Inspired by California's beach homes, the interior design is a mix of contemporary architecture and elements from the 1950s. Colors and textiles such as linen were chosen to evoke comfort and freshness, and wooden furniture and vintage accessories add an element of the elegance of age.

The use of materials such as natural stone and concrete walls with a wood grain finish help mitigate the heat, reducing the need for air conditioning. The concrete was employed mainly at the front of the residence, with a vertical garden installation that gives a fresh, natural appearance. Rooftop gardens were created because there is a multilevel building next to the back of the house, and it was important for the roof to be integrated into the landscape and provide a pleasant view for the neighboring building's users.

The main objective was to create multifunctional spaces within the house that would open to the view. To accomplish this, both levels of the home feature areas with floor-to-ceiling windows that lead to terraces. The house has a gym, a home cinema, two Jacuzzis, a pool with a terrace, a fireplace, living room, and dining room, as well as eight bedrooms that welcome the outdoors into the heart of the residence.

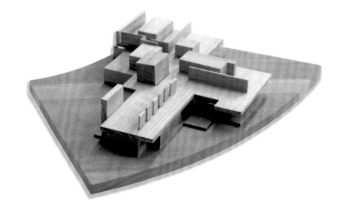

Mexico City, Mexico

Los Angeles, California

Milan, Italy

Ezequiel Farca / Founder +
Cristina Grappin / Partner

Collaborators

Clarissa Acevedo, Dinorah Acevedo, Michelle Alfaro, Gabriela Barrera, Liliana Barrientos, Felipe Beltrán, Margot Betech, Angelique Bidet, Martina Bobadilla, Estelle Bordas, Víctor Burgos, Analí Cabrera, Carlos Candia, Paulina Carlos, Javier Caro, Estefanía Carrete, Paola Castanedo, César Castello, César Castilla, Ian Castillo, Mariano Castillo, Sergio Castrejón, Julio Cedillo, Emillie Cohen, Sergio Cruz, María Fernanda de la Mora, Alejandra Díaz de León, Emilio Diaz, Tomás Díaz, Carlos Edeza, Erik Espinosa, Susana Fernández, Gerardo Frutos, Tamara García, Diana Gobea, Nohemí González, Roberto Gutiérrez, Amaranta Guzmán, Diego Guzmán, Emmanuel Hernández, Rubén Hernández, Xóchitl Juárez, Carlos Lara, César Lima, Víctor Lima, Germán Lomelí, Manuel López, Ximena Magaña, Etzully Maldonado, Adria Martínez, José Luis Martínez, Carlos Mena, Daniela Motta, Marcela Muñoz, Claudia Nava, Javier Núñez, Marco Orozco, Alonso Pérez, Edmar Pineda, Miguel Piña, Viridiana Quintana, Jorge Quiroga, Brenda Ramírez, Georgia Rivera, Fernanda Rodríguez, José Antonio Sánchez, Michaela Stachova, Adrián Suárez, Yazmín Suárez, Alejandra Téllez, Ana Torres, Roberto Valdez, Daniel Valero, Elder Willet, Ana Zatarain.

www.farcagrappin.com

First published in the United States of America in 2019 by
Rizzoli Electa
A Division of Rizzoli International Publications, Inc.
300 Park Avenue South
New York, NY 10010
www.rizzoliusa.com

Copyright © 2019 Ezequiel Farca + Cristina Grappin
Foreword: Paola Lenti
Text: Philip Jodidio
Interview: Michael Webb

Publisher: Charles Miers
Associate Publisher: Margaret Chace
Editor: Ellen R. Cohen
Production Manager: Colin Hough-Trapp
Managing Editor: Lynn Scrabis
Art Direction: Paloma Villamil Ríos
Collaborators: Ana Zatarain, César Castilla, Javier
Nuñez, Sofia Broid

Every effort has been made to acknowledge the
architects' and contributors' names for each project.
Any errors and omissions are unintentional and should
be notified to the architects, who will arrange for
corrections to appear in any reprints.

Printed in Italy

2019 2020 2021 2022 2023 / 10 9 8 7 6 5 4 3 2 1

ISBN 978-0-8478-6351-8
Library of Congress Control Number: 2019939187

Visit us online:
Facebook.com/RizzoliNewYork
Twitter: @Rizzoli_Books
Instagram.com/RizzoliBooks
Pinterest.com/RizzoliBooks
Youtube.com/user/RizzoliNY
Issuu.com/Rizzoli